www.arielmotor.co.uk

Picture Credits
t=top, tr=top right, tl=top left, bl= bottom left, br=bottom right, b=bottom

Ends Page: Audi Motors (l); KTM Sportcar GmbH (r); Ariel Motor Company Ltd (b)

P5: Gumpert; P6: Gumpert; P7: KTM Sportcar GmbH; P8: Daimler AG; P9: Daimler AG (b); P9: Daimler AG (t);
P10: Porsche Cars North America, Inc; P11: Porsche Cars North America, Inc (t); P11: Porsche Cars North America, Inc
(b); P12: Tesla Motors; P13: Tesla Motors; P14: Ariel Motor Company Ltd; P15: Ariel Motor Company Ltd (t),
P15: Ariel Motor Company Ltd (b);
P20: Bugatti Automibiles S.A.S; P21: Bugatti Automibiles S.A.S; P22: SSC; P23: SSC (tr); P24: RoadRazer Car
Company (tr); P24: RoadRazer Car Company (b); P25: RoadRazer Car Company (t); P25: RoadRazer Car Company (b);
P26: Courtesy Mercedes-Benz; P27: Courtesy Mercedes-Benz (tr); P27: Courtesy Mercedes-Benz (b); P28: Courtesy
Mercedes-Benz; P29: Courtesy Mercedes-Benz; P30: Courtesy Mercedes-Benz; P31: Courtesy Mercedes-Benz (br);
P32: Gumpert; P33: Gumpert (bl); P33: Gumpert (tr); P34: ArtegaGT (t); P34: ArtegaGT (b); P35: ArtegaGT (t);
P35: ArtegaGT (b); P37: General Motors (b); P39: KTM Sportcar GmbH (b); P39: KTM Sportcar GmbH (tl); P40: Audi
Motors (bl); P41: Audi Motors; P41: Audi Motors (tl);
P43: Ariel Motor Company Ltd (b); P44: ArtegaGT (b); P45: RoadRazer Car Company (tr);
P45: KTM Sportcar GmbH (br).

Published By: Robert Frederick Ltd.
4 North Parade, Bath, BA1 1LF, UK

First Published: 2009

Printed in China.

CONTENTS

About Cars 6

Smart Fortwo 8

Porsche 959 10

Tesla Roadster 12

Ariel Atom 500 14

Ferrari Enzo 16

Lamborghini Gallardo LP560-4 18

Bugatti Veyron 20

Ultimate Aero TT 22

The RoadRazer 24

Mercedes-Benz F400 26

SLK 55 AMG 28

Mercedes-Benz SLR McLaren 30

Gumpert Apollo 32

Artega GT 34

Hummer HX 36

KTM X-Bow 38

Audi R8 40

Facts and Records 42

Glossary 44

Index 45

ABOUT CARS

Karl Benz invented the first car in 1885. This car had three wheels and was powered by a petrol engine.

What's in this book?

Since then cars have evolved into the four wheeled wonders of today, where cars of many different shapes and sizes are available. This book will introduce you to three main types of amazing cars.

Street Cars

As the name suggests, street cars are utility vehicles that operate on roads. With rising oil prices, automobile companies are increasingly looking to more economical and smaller street cars to meet demand.

Sports Cars

Sports cars typically have lowered suspension, powerful engines and a streamlined body. They are designed for high speeds and good cornering, usually with stiffer suspension.

Super Cars

Super cars are high end sports cars with extremely powerful engines. They are designed for speed and performance and are luxury items that usually come with a hefty price tag!

Cars today are ever more daring and unique in their design.

Did You Know?

Almost 100,000 patents have been registered by inventors in the evolutionary history of the car.

Performance cars stand out with their sleek and aerodynamic designs.

SMART FORTWO

They say that good things come in small packages. The Smart Fortwo is a perfect example of this.

Two Seater

The Smart Fortwo is a smart and compact two-seater car. The car was first displayed at the 1998 Paris Motor Show. At the time, the car was named the City Coupe. The car was **modified** and relaunched as a second generation in early 2008.

 The compact design of the Fortwo means it can zip through small spaces.

Fits Anywhere

The Smart Fortwo is 2.69 metres (m) long, equal to the width of a truck or a regular parking slot. This means that two or three Smarts can park side by side in a standard space reserved for a single car. This ability to fit in tight spaces alone means that the car is perfect for crowded city roads.

Did You Know?

The Fortwo is made of interchangeable body panels — so one car can easily assume a different look.

TECHNICAL INFO

Manufacturer: Smart
Type: Microcar
Engine: 1,000cc
0-60 mph: 10.9 sec
Top speed: 90 mph

Sturdy Engine

The Smart Fortwo features an 84 bhp engine that powers the car from 0–60 mph in 10.9 seconds. The car can run for 60 miles on just 5.7 litres of petrol. The car comes with an automated 5-speed transmission. This means it can be operated manually or automatically, and even has a Formula One-style paddle gear change option.

The Smart Fortwo features a compact engine mounted in the rear of the car.

PORSCHE 959

The Porsche 959 was the first production car in history to reach 60 mph in under 4 seconds. It can be said that this model paved the way for the modern supercars.

Only limited numbers of the 959 were ever built.

The Perfect Car

The Porsche 959 was manufactured from 1986 to 1989, first as a rally car then as a street car. The car was described as the fastest, most technologically advanced sports car in history at the time. Only a limited number of the street-legal version were to be produced and today they are among the most collectible sports cars.

Did You Know?

The Porsche 959 was one of the first cars to have an all-wheel drive system.

Powerful Engine

For the 959, Porsche developed an existing engine and came up with a monster that turned out 450 horse power (hp) with a turbocharged flat-6. The engine was powerful enough to power the car to 60 mph in just 3.8 seconds, and on to a maximum speed of 197 mph.

 The powerful engine of the 959 was mounted in the rear of the car.

Muscular Design

The 959 had a muscular body with an ultra wide tail. A large **spoiler** at the rear gave downforce at high speeds. Aluminum, carbon fibre and other lightweight materials were used for the body. The wheels even had hollow spokes in an attempt to reduce weight!

TECHNICAL INFO
Manufacturer: Porsche
Car type: Sports car
Engine: 2,851cc
0-60 mph: 3.8 sec
Top speed: 197 mph

 The all-wheel drive system was originally developed for the rally version of the 959.

TESLA ROADSTER

Imagine a sports car that runs only on electricity and releases no harmful gasses! The Tesla Roadster is the answer.

Electrifying Car

The Tesla Roadster is a high performance, electric sports car manufactured by Tesla Motors. This attractive-looking roadster was designed with the help of Lotus. The body of the car is designed in a special way to maximise efficiency and performance, using a structure made of carbon fibre and aluminium. For a jerk-free ride, Tesla has only two gears. It also has electrically controlled door handles, **airbags** and **anti-lock braking system**.

Did You Know?

The first known electric locomotive was built by Scottish inventor Robert Davidson in 1837.

 The Tesla is based on a modified Lotus Elise body that was redesigned by Lotus engineers.

No Engine

As an electric car, the Tesla Roadster doesn't have an internal combustion engine. Instead, it has the Energy Storage System (ESS) which comprises of a 450 kg lithium ion battery. The 6,831 cells in the battery pack are enough to produce over 248 hp. The Tesla can cover around 240 miles without recharging. The lack of an engine means that the car is very silent.

Dream Machine

The Tesla breaks all the conventional images of an electric car with a smooth, sleek body. The car is fast and stylish, performing and handling like a sports car.

TECHNICAL INFO
Manufacturer: Tesla Motors
Car type: Roadster
0-60 mph: 3.9 sec
Top speed: 125 mph
(electronically limited)

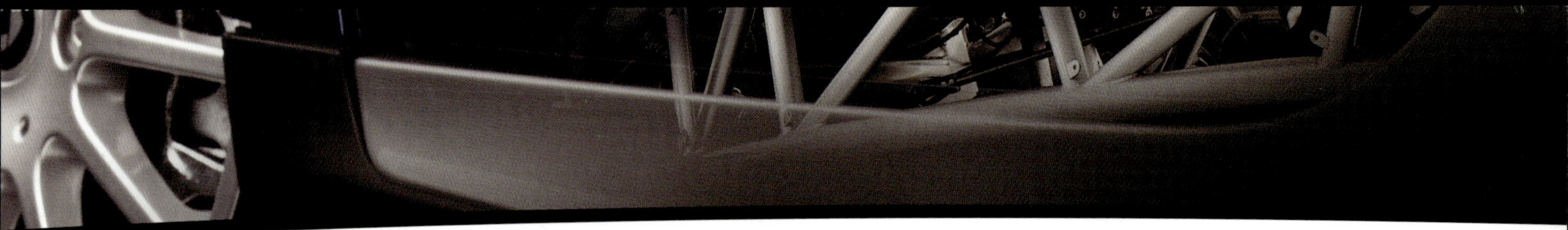

ARIEL ATOM 500

A sports car that has an inside-out look! The Ariel Atom 500's basic body structure is unlike any other sports car that you will have seen before.

www.arielmotor.co.uk

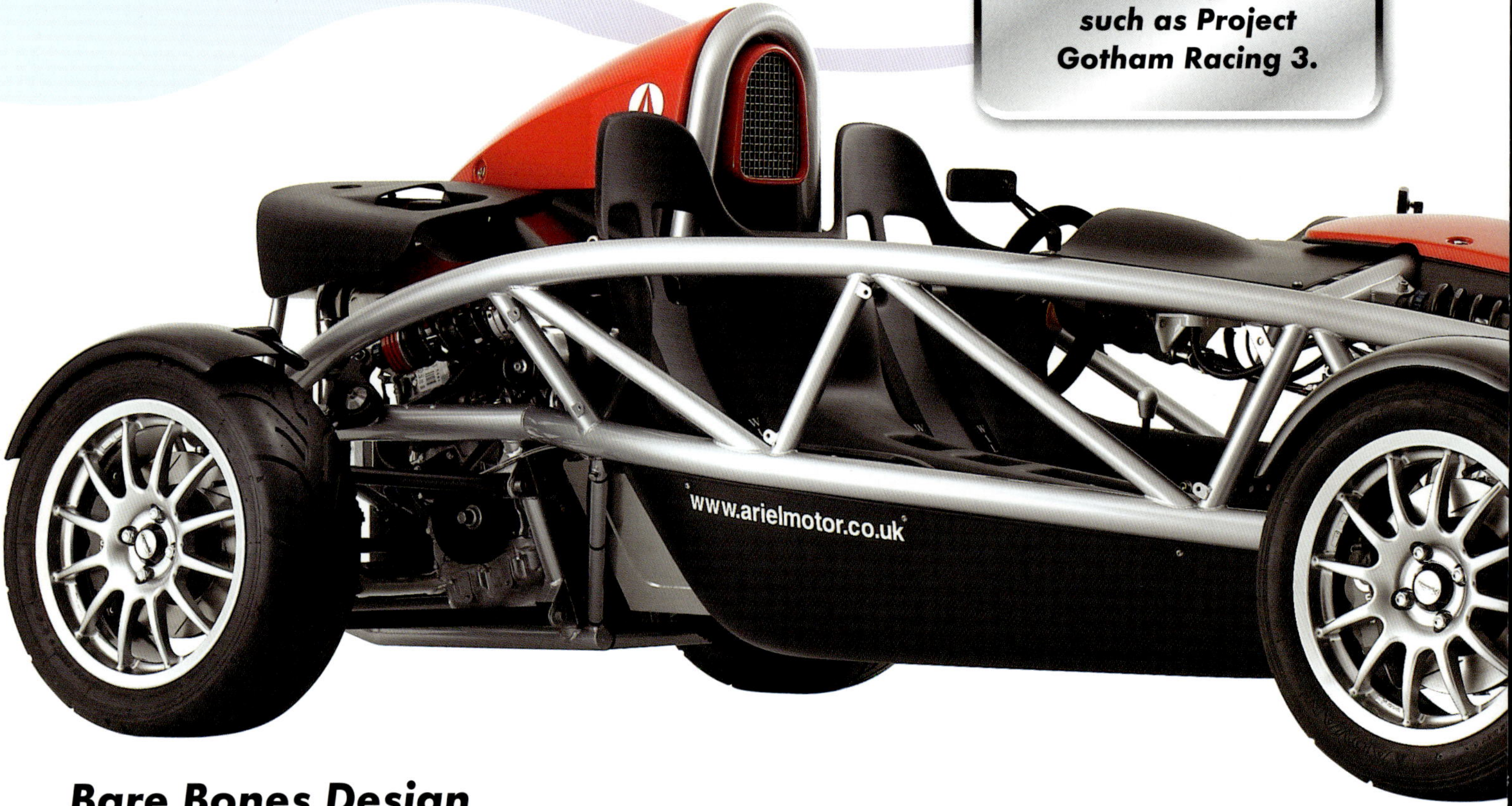

Bare Bones Design

The Ariel Atom is produced by England's Ariel Motor Company, and manufactured under license in USA by TMI Auto Tech Inc. With Formula One racing car looks, the Ariel Atom has a nose cone and an engine mounted just behind the driver. There are no doors, no roof and no windshield – so hold on to your hats!

Mean Machine

The Ariel Atom is available with a range of engine options, most notably the supercharged Honda Civic Type-R K20 and the General Motors Ecotec engine. The car's top speed is relatively tame compared to other sports cars. However, the lightweight design means the car is capable of tremendous acceleration. Moreover, rigid suspension allows for tight and fast cornering. What little bodywork there is comes in the form of separate panels. This reduces weight and the cost and allows for easy maintenance.

The engine is housed right behind the seating compartment.

The car can be described as no frills: it doesn't even have a stereo!

TECHNICAL INFO

Manufacturer: Ariel Motor Company

Car type: Sports car

Engine: 1,988 cc

0-60 mph: 2.9 sec

Top speed: 140 mph

www.arielmotor.co.uk

FERRARI ENZO

The Ferrari Enzo is a two-seater, 12 cylinder min-engine berlinetta, named after the company's founder, Enzo Ferrari. Built in 2002, it has a carbon-fiber body, electrohydraulic shift transmission and ceramic composite disc brakes. Only 400 models of this car were ever made.

Power

The Ferrari Enzo has a V12 engine. This enables the car to reach a top speed of over 350 km/h. The 660hp engine can power the car from 0.62 mph in just 3.65 seconds.

TECHNICAL INFO

Manufacturer: Ferrari
Car Type: Road-going Supercar
Engine: 5998.80cc
0-60mph: 3.65 sec
Top Speed: Over 350 km/h

In the Lap of Luxury

The Ferrari Enzo has carbon-fiber seats, which could be ordered in a variety of sizes and positions to fit the driver. It also boasts F1 style switches and controls on the dashboard. Ferrari's goal was to create a road-going supercar with the same "human-machine interface" that had been developed for the track.

Did You Know?

The Ferrari Enzo weighs 1,255kg. The Enzo typically trades above £800,000 at auction.

LAMBORGHINI GALLARDO LP560-4

The Lamborghini Gallardo is one of Lamborghini's most produced models to date, with over 10,000 built in the first 7 years. The Lamborghini Gallardo combines fun driving with safety. Named after a famous breed of fighting bull, the V-10 Gallardo has been Lamborghini's sales leader.

LP560-4

The LP560-4 was first presented in 2008, it is powered by a 5.2,L V-10 engine. It features a direct fuel injection system to improve efficiency, fuel consumption and also helps to reduce CO_2 emissions.

The Power

The 5.2L, V-10 engine is more powerful then any of Lamborghini's previous cars. This enables the car to reach a top speed of 202 mph . The 552 hp engine can power the car from 0-60 mph in 3.7 seconds. It comes with 2 transmission choices, 6-speed manual or 6-speed E gear.

Did You Know?

The rear spoiler is electronically controlled and rises at speed to enhance traction.

 The Lamborghini Gallardo is an amazing car, stylish, powerful and superb to drive.

And the Style

A new grouping of sharp triangular and trapezoidal forms, highlighted in body colour and black, give the Gallardo LP560-40 a broader and more serious look. It has 19 inch matte black aluminum wheels with polished silver spokes.

BUGATTI VEYRON

Bugatti is one of the automotive industry's oldest brand names. Today the company is owned by Volkswagen and manufactures one of the fastest sports car in the world, the Bugatti Veyron.

Did You Know?

At full throttle the Veyron does just 2.46 miles per gallon of fuel!

The Bugatti Veyron

Volkswagen wanted to develop the most powerful car in the world. So they took a 1,001 hp engine and designed a car around it. Under the sleek body are the kinds of features more commonly seen on Formula One cars. Front and rear spoilers provide better control. Roof-mounted snorkels, the rear-deck vents and side-mounted scoops bring air to the engine and rear brakes.

The Veyron has the greatest acceleration of any production car ever made.

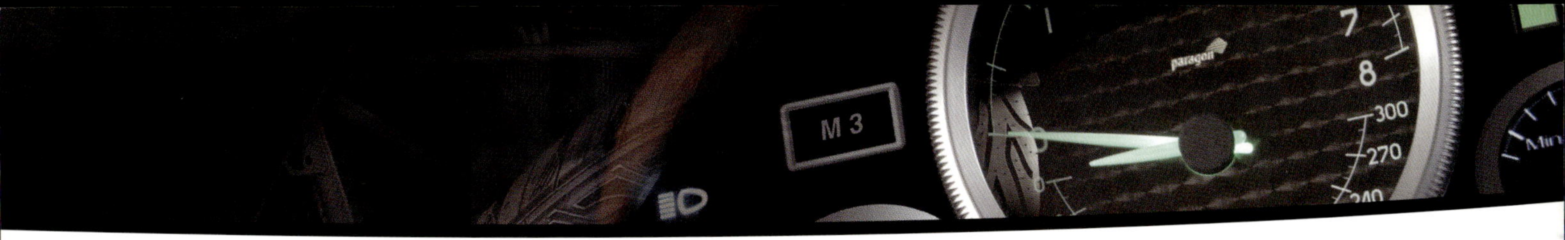

Engine

The Veyron has a massive 16-cylinder engine that delivers 1,001 **horsepower**. The engineers came up with a unique W-shaped design that allowed them to pack a lot of power into a compact design. To keep its weight down, the engine is made of aluminium and magnesium and has four turbochargers. The 7-gear system is computer-controlled, like those found in a Formula One car. There is no clutch pedal or shift lever — the computer controls the clutch disks as well as the actual shifting.

 Almost every part of the Veyron's interior is covered in rich leather.

Interiors

The Veyron is a two seater, but it seats the two people in lavish style. The interior is covered almost completely in leather, from the dash to the doors. Only the instruments and a few metal details interrupt the opulent trim. The car also surrounds its occupants with every sort of electronic gadget, from a remarkable stereo system to a **navigation system**.

TECHNICAL INFO
Manufacturer: Volkswagen
Car type: Super car
Engine: 7,993cc
0-60 mph: 2.46 sec
Top speed: 253 mph

SSC ULTIMATE AERO TT

On September 13, 2007, the Ultimate Aero TT hit a top speed of 257 mph, making it the world's fastest production car!

Features

The Aero's body is made of carbon fibre and titanium to help reduce the weight of the car while keeping it strong. The car has a leather interior, 10-speaker system, a camera to assist with reversing, and even a hydraulic lift to help the car get over speed bumps!

Did You Know?

The SSC Ultimate Aero TT is one of the most powerful road cars in the world.

The Ultimate Aero produces more emissions-legal horsepower than any other production car in the world.

Engine

The Aero has a massive 6.35 litre engine with a **displacement** of 6,345cc that produces 1,183 hp. The engine is twin-turbocharged, with a driver-operated boost.

THE ROADRAZER

The first thing that you will notice about the RoadRazer is its long snout. This two-seater car, which weighs just 300 kg, is one of the lightest road-legal sports cars available.

With its pointed nose cone the RoadRazer looks amazingly shark-like.

The Design

The RoadRazer was created by Mikkel Steen Pedersen, a motor racing enthusiast and engineer. The RoadRazer promises to deliver stunning levels of performance, thanks to the car's power-to-weight ratio, low centre of gravity and effective **aerodynamics**.

Engine

The RoadRazer has a converted 1,300**cc** Suzuki Hayabusa motorcycle engine. The engine produces approximately 175 hp, hitting 60 mph in just 3 seconds. Unlike most wet sump car engines, the RoadRazer has a dry sump oil pumping system.

TECHNICAL INFO
Manufacturer: RoadRazer
Car type: Sports car
Engine: 1,300cc
0-60 mph: 3 sec

The engine is rear-mounted, behind the tandem passenger seat.

Exterior and Interior

The RoadRazer has a racing seat for the driver positioned very close to the ground, like a true racing car. There is a passenger seat, but this is in a tandem arrangement just behind the driver, with the passenger placing their legs either side of the seat in front; not recommended for long journeys!

The raised nosecone position of the RoadRazer is designed not only to aid performance in cornering, but also to assist with day-to-day driving when parking and clearing speed-bumps etc. The curved side pods of the RoadRazer act like inverted aeroplane wings, pushing the car into the ground and affording grip and handling.

The car seats two people one behind the other, but the passenger must straddle the driver's seat with their legs!

MERCEDES-BENZ F 400

The Mercedes-Benz F 400 Carving is a concept car and research vehicle. Among several innovations, the car gets the last part of its name because of its ability to tilt its wheels inwards when cornering, carving like a ski or snowboard.

Design

The Carving is a triumph of innovative design and style. The engineers have mixed steel, aluminium and carbon fibre to make the car lightweight and yet sturdy. Perhaps the most distinctive elements of the design are the wing profile wheel arches that flare out to allow for the wheels to tilt in cornering.

Did You Know?

The Carving uses new lighting technology: fibre optic wires transmit light from special lamps beneath the bonnet to the main headlamps.

Active Camber Control System

The system of tilting the F 400's wheels inwards when cornering is known as active camber control. According to Mercedes, this system gives 30 percent more lateral stability than conventional turning. The system is controlled by a computer that monitors driver inputs to the steering and will adjust the tilt, or camber, of the tyres automatically as needed to maximise grip and increase safety.

 When the car is cornering, the outer wheels tilt inwards, leaving only the inner area of these tyres in contact with the road.

 The car has the extended bonnet and short tail end of a classic roadster, but that's where the similarities end!

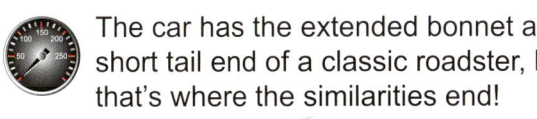

SLK 55 AMG

The Mercedes-Benz SLK 55 AMG is a stylish, high-performance roadster, having been tuned and modified from the standard SLK 55.

Powerhouse

Underneath the bonnet the SLK 55 AMG has a supercharged 5.5 litre V8 engine powering the car. The power is harnessed by a 7-speed gearbox controlled by shift paddles on the steering wheel. The car boasts the only V8 engine in its class and is capable of up to 6,700 rpm.

Did You Know?

AMG began tuning Mercedes cars over 30 years ago, before they were bought by the company.

Interiors and Exteriors

The SLK 55 AMG can be converted into a coupe from a convertible and vice versa at the push of a button. The roof neatly folds away in just 16 seconds! Inside, the car comes with contoured sports seats in fine leather, as well as an ergonomically designed steering wheel, complete with paddle gear shift.

The cabin of the SLK 55 AMG

Safety First

AMG has gone to great lengths to ensure that the car is safer, quicker and cleaner than its predecessors. It has also worked at improving the aerodynamics of the car. Handling is assisted by state-of-the-art active body control, while high-performance disc brakes are fitted to both front and rear wheels.

TECHNICAL INFO

Manufacturer: Mercedes-Benz

Car type: Convertible

Engine: 5,439cc

0-60 mph: 4.8 sec

Top speed: 155 mph (electronically limited)

MERCEDES-BENZ SLR MCLAREN

As the name suggests the SLR McLaren is Formula One inspired in both its performance and its styling – indeed SLR stands for sport, light, racing! Ultimate performance and detailed styling combine to make the fastest road-legal convertible available today.

The SLR has a 21st century take on the gullwing doors from the original Mercedes 300SL.

Amazing Roof System

Perhaps the most attractive feature of this roadster is the roof system. It has a z-fold roof which opens and closes in just 10 seconds. The roof is made from special hi-tech material that is designed to withstand the force created at high speeds, while insulating the cabin from the elements and noise.

Aerodynamics

The SLR features active aerodynamics. There is a spoiler mounted on the rear which automatically raises at speeds above 60 mph. This increases the downforce, helping to pin the rear of the car to the ground at high speeds.

Design

The SLR McLaren uses Triax carbon fibre for the body of the car. The brakes of the car are made of carbon ceramic that provide for optimum performance and control under braking. In the cockpit, carbon fibre and luxurious leather combine to evoke the feel of SLRs from previous decades.

GUMPERT APOLLO

The Gumpert Apollo is a road-legal high-performance sports car. The designers' vision was to produce a car with so much downforce, power and aerodynamic efficiency that it could technically drive upside-down!

Road Car Meets Track Car

The Gumpert Apollo is the perfect synthesis of a road vehicle and track car. According to the makers, the car generates a sense of passion and pleasure beyond all expectations. Noticeable racing-inspired features include the front lip air splitter and and roof-mounted triangular air intake.

TECHNICAL INFO
Manufacturer: Gumpert
Car type: Super car
Engine: 4,163cc
0-60 mph: 3.0 sec
Top speed: 224 mph

Interiors

The inside of the Gumpert Apollo is compact and designed to be lightweight. The customer is then able to specify the interior features as they please. Options include air conditioning, music system and a backward facing camera to help with reversing. Seats are individually tailored to the customer with padding, upholstery and adjustable paddles. Every detail, right down to the colour of the seams and stitching, can be specified by the customer!

 The interior of the car is functional and lightweight.

Features

The Apollo has an Audi 4.2 litre V8 engine combined with a six-speed gearbox. The engine produces a respectable 650 hp that powers the car from 0-60 mph in just 3 seconds. A fibre glass frame and carbon fibre body panels mean that the car weighs in at just 1,200 kg. The car's wide and imposing wheel arches house impressive 19-inch aliminium-cast wheel rims.

 The Gumpert Apollo is built around an Audi V8 engine.

ARTEGA GT

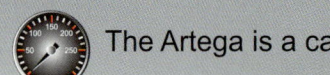

The Artega GT is a mid-engined sports car designed by Henrik Fisker of Aston Martin DB9 fame. This compact car weighs only 1,100 kg, giving it an excellent power-to-weight ratio.

The Artega is a car with attitude!

Agility, driving dynamics and safety were key factors in the design of the car.

Engine

The Artega is powered by a 3.6-litre Volkswagen-sourced V-6 engine. The engine produces 300 hp of power with a top speeds of 167 mph. **Acceleration** from 0-60 mph is expected to be under five seconds. The engine is placed horizontally in the rear.

Design

The hood and the headlights of the Artega GT stand out for their broad and distinctive design. The interior of the Artega is surprisingly spacious for a GT with its kind of power. Indeed, Artega boast that their car is the width of a luxury limousine!

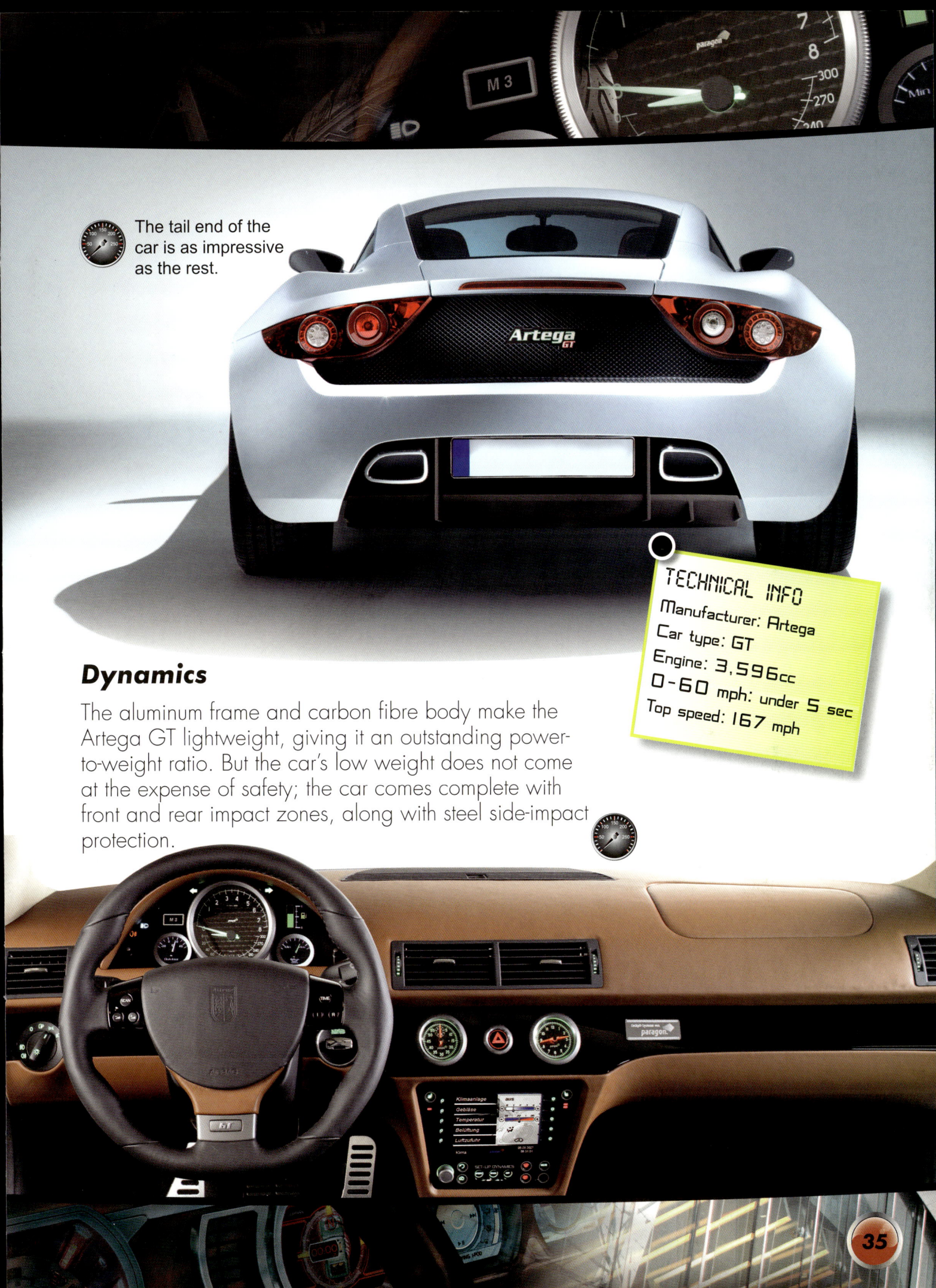

The tail end of the car is as impressive as the rest.

TECHNICAL INFO
Manufacturer: Artega
Car type: GT
Engine: 3,596cc
0-60 mph: under 5 sec
Top speed: 167 mph

Dynamics

The aluminum frame and carbon fibre body make the Artega GT lightweight, giving it an outstanding power-to-weight ratio. But the car's low weight does not come at the expense of safety; the car comes complete with front and rear impact zones, along with steel side-impact protection.

HUMMER HX

The Hummer HX is a concept sports utility vehicle (SUV), based on the larger Hummer already in production. This tank-like vehicle is definitely not sleek or small, but is actually a more compact 2-door version of its big brother!

The Powerhouse

The Hummer HX is powered by a 3.6 litre V6 engine that produces 304 horsepower. A four-wheel drive system delivers this power to the wheels for high-performance off-roading.

The sloping rear roof of the HX can be easily detached.

The exterior of the HX retains many design elements from the Hummer.

Did You Know?

The roof and doors can also be easily removed.

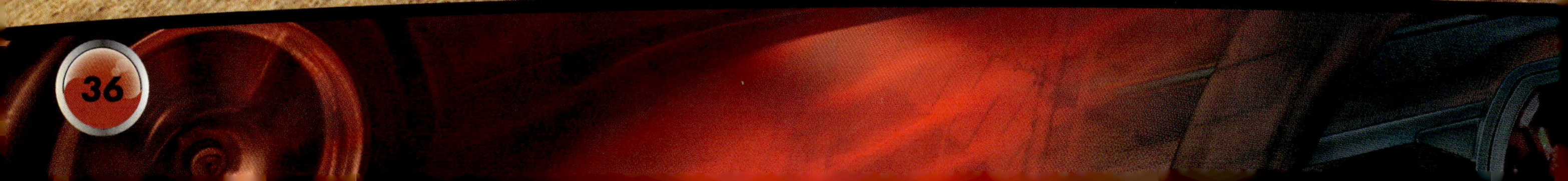

Interiors

The Hummer HX has no grand interior, but is designed, instead, to be practical and functional. The insides are made up of aluminium and there is carpet flooring. The seats are lightweight and compact. The three pods by the steering wheel contain LCD screens. The seats are constructed from lightweight material and come complete with 4-point racing-style seatbelts.

Newbie Designers

The design of the HX was driven by input from three young designers who were new to GM and the Hummer design studio. But the car retains classic Hummer design elements including the round headlamps in square housings, an upright windshield, hood vents and prominent air intakes.

The HX's interior is functional and robust with exposed metalwork.

TECHNICAL INFO
Manufacturer: Hummer
Car type: SUV
Engine: 3,564cc

KTM X-BOW

The KTM X-Bow is the first car to be produced by motorcycle manufacturers KTM. By the maker's own admission, the X-Bow is an aggressively designed, radical, lightweight sports car.

Light But Fast

The X-Bow is powered by a 240 hp Audi TFSI engine that powers the car from 0-60 mph in just 3.9 seconds. The relatively small engine is capable of this because the car itself weighs in at just 790 kgs. This four-wheel pocket rocket is 144.5 inches long, 73.6 inches wide and just 45.7 inches high!

Features

The KTM X-Bow doesn't have a roof, or even a windscreen, so a helmet is adviseable! The manufacturer has tried to develop a vehicle that combines the thrills of both bikes and cars. Built on the principles of racing technology, the wheels stand clear from the chassis, with exposed racing suspension. So stripped back and prepared for racing is this car that it doesn't even have any doors – you simply climb over the side to get in!

Did You Know?

The KTM X-Bow is made with Austrian design and money, a German engine, and Italian engineering.

Interiors

The interior of the X-Bow is also functional for racing. You won't find any heavy and unnecessary luxuries here! There's no heating, or radio, or even an instrument panel! The shells of the seats are merged into the carbon fibre body. In place of a boot, there is a detachable storage box.

Driver information such as speed and fuel level is provided via an electronic screen.

TECHNICAL INFO

Manufacturer: KTM
Car type: Racing
Engine: 2,000cc
0-60 mph: 3.9 sec

AUDI R8

The Audi R8 is an exciting and high-performance mid-engined super car. Borrowing some of its styling from Lamborghini, the R8 is a bold statement from Audi.

Cockpit Interior

The R8 is a 2-seater sports car with a luxurious interior. The sports seats are specially designed and finished in leather. Leather trim continues on the doors and dashboard. The R8 even comes with the option of a specially designed Bang & Olufsen sound system.

The R8 was awarded Best Handling Car of 2007 by Autocar magazine.

Powerful Engine

The R8 has a powerful 4.2 litre V8. Even at low speeds, the powerplant gives it a higher manoeuverability. The engine can power the car from 0-60 mph in just 4.4 seconds. The all-wheel drive system is controlled by Audi's R-tronic **gear box**. The six-speed gear box is controlled by a conventional stick-shift or by the paddles on the steering wheel. The car also has the option of **ceramic brakes**.

TECHNICAL INFO

Manufacturer: Audi
Car type: Sports
Engine: 4,163cc
0 - 60 mph: 4.4 sec
Top speed: 187 mph

FACTS AND RECORDS

Henry Ford, founder of the Ford Motor Company, started producing his famous Ford Model T cars in 1908. Early Ford cars were available only in black.

In 1916, 55 per cent of the cars in the world were Model T Fords. This is a record that has never been broken.

The first patent for seat belts was granted to Edward J. Claghorn of New York on February 10, 1885.

In 1923, women were responsible for 173 new car-related inventions. Among these inventions were a carburetor and an electric engine starter.

A car, when modified by either altering its performance or by altering the design, is known as a custom car. The trend of customizing cars started in the mid 20th century in America and in this period the customizing process became known as 'hot rodding'.

Custom cars have appeared in many Hollywood movies and popular television series. The famous Batmobile used in the 1966 TV series was designed around Ford's concept car, the Lincoln Futura.

The Bugatti Veyron is the world's most expensive street-legal supercar on the market today.

On the racing track, different coloured flags are used to signal specific messages: a yellow flag is waved for caution and danger ahead; a red-and-yellow striped flag is waved for oil on track; red signals the race must stop; while a black-and-white chequered flag is waved as the cars cross the finishing line.

In 2006, Japan produced 9.75 million cars, more than any other country.

The world's fastest biofuel super car is the Koenigsegg CCXR, which is designed to run on ethanol-based fuels.

The Bugatti Veyron takes ten seconds to stop from its top speed of 253 mph.

GLOSSARY

Acceleration: The increase in the rate of speed of something

Aerodynamic: A shape that helps reduce the drag caused by air moving past it

Air bag: A safety device fitted to cars that deploys a bag of air rapidly upon impact

Anti-lock Braking System: A system that transmits driver pressure on the brake pedal in a way that stops tyres from locking up

Cc: Cubic centimetre: a metric unit of measurement used in relation to the size of a vehicle's engine

Ceramic brakes: High-performance disc brakes that can endure high temperatures and levels of wear

Coupe: A car with two doors and a fixed roof

Emissions: Gasses that are produced by the combustion engine and released through the exhaust

Gear box: An assembly of cogs that help transfer power from the engine to the wheels of a vehicle at a range of speeds

Horsepower (hp): A measurement of power

Navigation System: An electronic map with route instructions

Powerplant: The engine of a vehicle

Sensotronic Brake Control System: A brake system that works electronically

Spoiler: A long and narrow plate on the upper surface of the rear part of the car giving downforce to the rear wheels at high speed

Suspension: The system of springs and shock absorbers by which a vehicle is cushioned from road conditions

INDEX

Acceleration 34
Active Camber Control System 27
Aerodynamic 24, 30, 31
All-wheel Drive System 10, 11, 41
Anti-lock Braking System 12

Benz, Karl 6
Bugatti, Ettore 18

Carbon Fibre 12, 19, 22, 24, 26, 32
Ceramic Brakes 41
Cockpit 29, 33, 35, 40

Electric Car 13

Energy Storage System 13
Equipment 39

Fisker, Henrik 34
Four-wheel Drive System 36

Gasoline 6, 9, 23,
Gearbox 19, 28, 32, 41
Gumpert, Roland 32

Hayabusa Engine 24, 25

Lateral Stability 27

Navigation System 21

Pedersen, Mikkel Steen 24
Powerplant 19, 35, 41

Sensotronic Brake Control System 28
Spoiler 11, 20, 30
Stereo System 21
SUV 36, 37

Turbocharger 21

USB Connector 37

Xenon Lamps 26

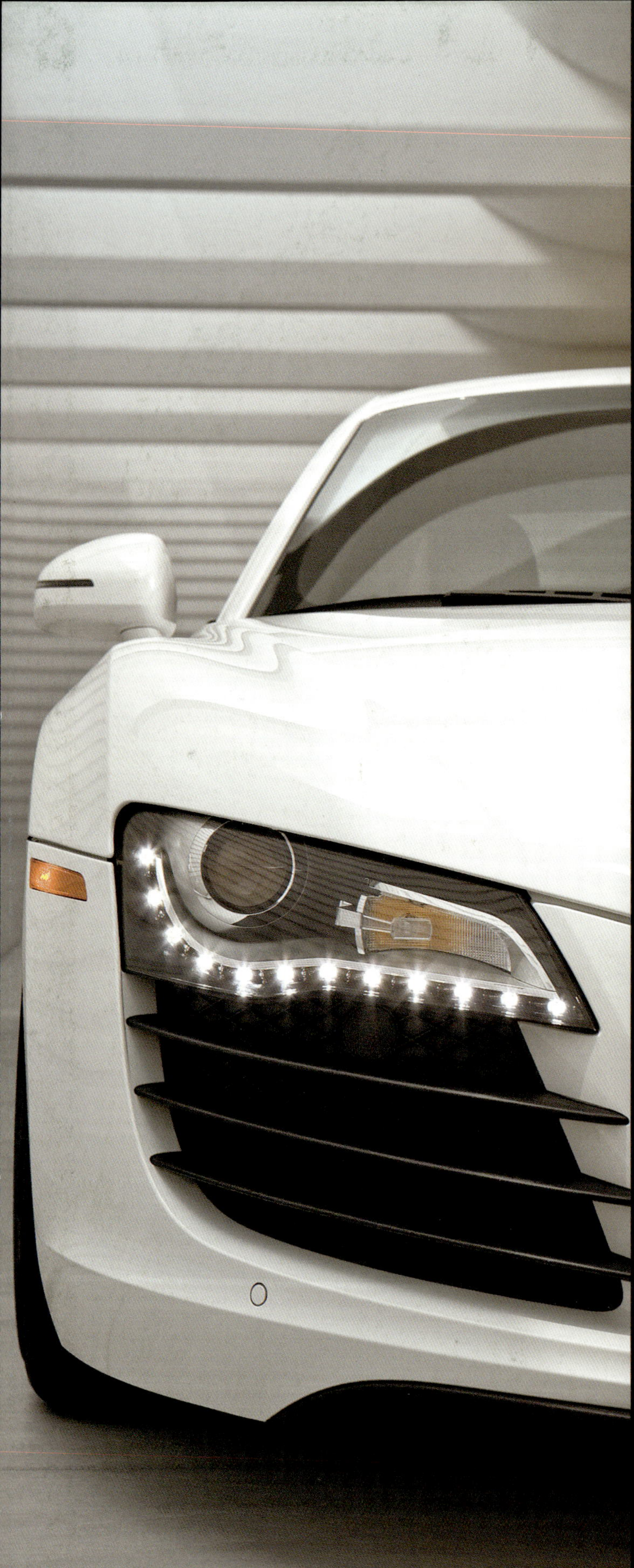

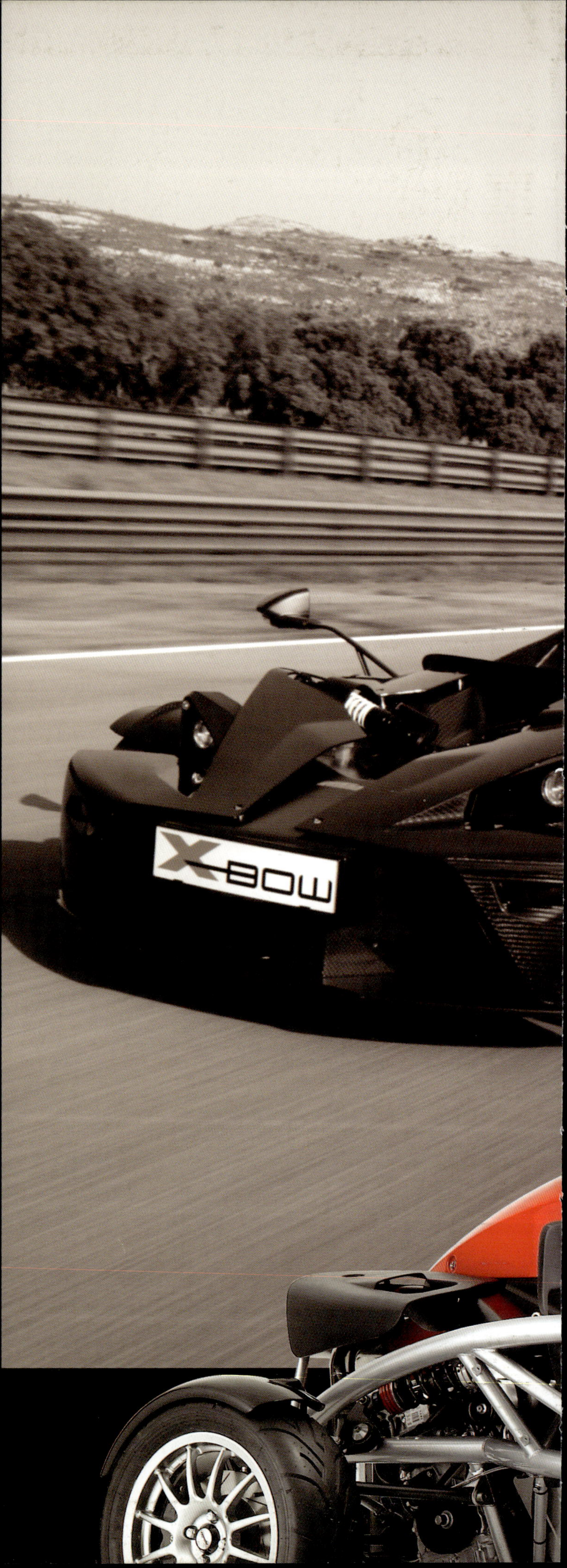
X-BOW